HALF THE MAN I USED TO BE

HALF THE MAN I USED TO BE

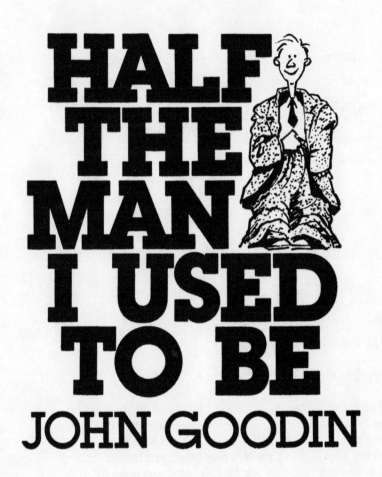

JOHN GOODIN

WORD PUBLISHING
Dallas · London · Sydney · Singapore

HALF THE MAN I USED TO BE

First published in the United States by Alive Publishing,
Raleigh, N.C. This revised and expanded 1990
edition published by Word Publishing, Dallas, Texas.

Printed in the United States of America

0 1 2 3 9   AGF   9 8 7 6 5 4 3 2 1

This book is dedicated to my wife,

SHELBA

to our sons,

MARK and SCOTT

and to the dear people in our church.
Their encouragement and support helped
make possible my weight loss and the
writing of this book.

Contents

I had the happiest plate in town!

Introduction

I was raised to be a fat person. As a youngster I was encouraged to have seconds and even thirds. My mom was a great cook; I loved to eat, so I was a willing subject. I ate "for all the starving children in China" at least seventy-two times. Not only did I always have a "happy plate," my plate was hilarious most of the time.

Finally, after a multitude of fad diets (and a million pills) I learned how to win this battle with fat. Over the years I must have tried a hundred diets. On some I lost weight, but I would always gain it back *plus* some. *Dieting* simply doesn't work. When you diet:

1) You're miserable, hungry and feel bad.

2) You're grouchy so no one else wants to be around you.

3) You strain to exercise willpower, often substituting all kinds of pills, potions, "milk shake" beverages and packaged foods for the real thing.

4) You finally reach (or come close) to your goal and say, "whew, now I can get back to normal again!"

5) You gain it all back plus some for good measure. A diet is that agonizing period of starvation just prior to a ten-pound weight gain.

Dieting is certainly immoral. Maybe it ought to be illegal. What do you think?

There Has to Be a Better Way!!

There is, and that's what this book is all about. This is not just another diet book. Apply the principles of this book to your life and you will become healthier and slimmer *and* enjoy life in the process . . . *it works!*

In my first full year of doing what I detail in this book I lost 123 pounds. I'm on my way to literally being *Half the Man I Used to Be.* I'm not hungry, do not feel deprived, don't count calories, feel great and I am enjoying life more than ever.

So, whether you need to lose 10 pounds or 200 pounds, you can do it safely without any gimmicks (pills, potions, "milk shake" beverages) or expensive packaged foods. *Interested?* Read on. By the way, this book is not only a book for you to enjoy and benefit from, it is also a workbook for you to use in becoming a slimmer, healthier you.

Agony's delight!!

HALF THE MAN I USED TO BE

Boy, are you fat!

1

Are You Motivated? Do You Really Want to Lose That Weight?

Little Children Tell the Truth

One Sunday morning a new family in the community visited our church. As the pastor, I certainly wanted them to feel welcome, so after the service I walked over to them to thank them for coming. Their three-year-old son, with a look of amazement on his face, blurted out at the top of his voice, "Boy, are you fat!" He had never seen anyone so large . . . I was huge. We all laughed (though we were embarrassed) and I started toward home thinking to myself, *The boy's right, I sure am fat; I need to do something to control it.* But I had already said that a thousand times over the years.

A "Revealing" Wedding Ceremony

Another time, I conducted a wedding ceremony for a young couple attending our church. I did not have anyone to assist me—just the young couple, the bridesmaids, the ushers and I were at the front of the church. I was wearing a clergyman's robe, and it was tight (I had to really suck in the gut just to zip it up). Everything went fine and I pronounced them husband and wife.

13

She thought "me" was "we."

During the reception I continued to wear the robe. A little elderly lady (who probably was a little nearsighted) spoke to me from across the room: "Dr. Goodin, you and your associate did a fine job marrying those young folks!" I was the only preacher within a mile . . . but she thought I was two people!

When you're big enough to be confused for two, it's time to do something about it!

Other Reasons Why I Wanted to Lose Weight

1) For the first time ever, my health was being noticeably affected by my being fat. At age forty-seven, hardly a kid any-more, my weight had ballooned to an incredible 400 pounds . . . the most I had ever weighed! Though I was six feet tall (with a large frame), I simply couldn't handle all the weight. I was suffer-ing from frequent headaches, had little energy, and generally just didn't feel as good as I once did. If I didn't do something soon, the excellent health I had known all my life would likely come crash-ing down.

2) I believed the best years of my marriage were yet to come. Shelba and I had been married twenty-seven years, we had two terrific grown sons, yet we were still in the prime of our lives. To enjoy those future years with Shelba I needed to be *alive* (of course), in good shape, and full of strength, energy, and stamina. To do that I had to bring my weight problem under control.

3) As a pastor, I needed to be a good example to our congregation *and* to those outside our church. I had been a poor example and it simply had to stop. I had greatly abused my temple of the Holy Spirit and this had to come to a screeching halt.

4) There were also a number of other smaller (but important) reasons:

a) During the preceding year or so I had developed a rather strange illness . . . I was *sick* of being fat.
b) I was tired of pants that ripped under the strain and shirts that gaped open.
c) I was tired of not being able to see my shoes unless I sucked in my gut and leaned over.
d) I was tired of requesting a table at a restaurant (I couldn't fit into a booth).
e) I was tired of having to ask for a seat belt extension in order to fasten my seat belt on an airplane. I was usually the only one *that fat* on the plane.
f) And finally I was tired of looking for the "Tent Size" department when I went to a clothing store.

So I Crawled out on a Limb . . . and Sawed It off behind Me!

I was on a Valentine's Day weekend retreat. The director of the retreat (Earl Tyson) asked me to "take a few minutes and speak to the folks." So I stood up before the group of approximately 125 people. Without any introductory comments, I made an unusual request: "Will all the fat people present please stand up?" For a few minutes people sat stunned, defining "fat" for themselves and deciding whether or not my request applied to

If you're fat, please stand up.

them. With varying degrees of shock and anger (the expressions on some faces were very interesting to say the least), people slowly began to stand up.

Fifty or more people finally got to their feet, and I proceeded to deliver a mini-sermon to them (*and to me*) challenging each of us to get our lives under control. I called upon each of us to lose weight: "Make this moment a public commitment to do so; a year from now let's be healthier, slimmer people!"

Everyone applauded and I sat down. "Dear Lord," I thought, "what have I done? There are five couples here from our church; they will be watching me in the months to come to see if I follow through. Boy, oh boy—I really did it this time . . . now I've got to follow through!" Incidentally, for the rest of the retreat everybody watched to see what I would eat. "Lord, Lord, what have I done?"

What am I doing out here?

Planning . . . a key to success.

2

Planning to Get Started

Get Real Honest with Yourself

I came home from the retreat and procrastinated for over a month. I was like the sign in the little country store: "FREE PEPSIS TOMORROW." Of course, "Tomorrow" never comes; if you want a Pepsi, you would have to buy it today. With every meal, *I remembered the retreat.* With every Sunday worship service, *I remembered the retreat.* With every contact with those couples who had gone with us, *I remembered the retreat . . . and on and on.*

Finally, I sat down to plan how to win the infamous "battle of the bulge":

1) The first thing I had to do was to *really* admit that I was *fat!* Fat people want to think of themselves in every other way:

YOU CAN CALL ME

OR YOU CAN CALL ME

"Chunky"

"Stout"

17

YOU CAN CALL ME

"Stocky"

OR YOU CAN CALL ME

"Big-boned"

YOU CAN CALL ME

"Large-framed"

OR YOU CAN CALL ME

"Plump"

YOU CAN CALL ME   OR

"Pleasingly Plump"   You can even call me "slightly overweight" . . .
                         BUT DON'T YOU DARE CALL ME FAT!

2) Second, I set a goal—what (how much) I wanted to lose and how soon I wanted to lose it. I set my goal: to lose 170 pounds. That would bring my weight down to 230 pounds, a good weight for me. At 230 pounds I would look slim (without even a spare tire) and feel great (in my Army days I was at that weight and in good shape). I didn't gain all my weight overnight and I knew I could not lose it overnight. Wanting to be reasonable, I gave myself twenty-four months to lose the weight; 170 pounds in twenty-four months—that could be done.

How about your goal? Take a moment and set it now; remember, "tomorrow" never comes.

My Goal:

I want to lose _____ pounds.
I want to lose it in _____ months.

(Be reasonable—give yourself plenty of time.)

3) Third, I listed my reasons for wanting to lose weight. My reasons are the ones, of course, that I discussed in detail in chapter 1 of this book. I listed them because I needed to see them in black and white. I needed them right in front of me reminding me of the urgency of the situation. I needed to be strongly motivated, and these reasons spelled out that motivation!

What is your motivation for losing weight—for becoming a slimmer, healthier you? I guarantee you that the motivation is present within you; you just need to bring it out by listing the reasons you want to lose weight. The very fact that you're reading this book indicates that you do indeed want to win the victory over fat.

Take a few minutes right now and list your reasons for wanting to lose weight. Some of your reasons will be similar to mine; some will be different. The important thing is that they are *your* reasons, and that you're getting them out right in front of you so you can act upon them. Your motivation will be spelled out in black and white.

List your reasons for losing weight on the chart on the next page.

Review these reasons often as you prepare to lose weight.

My Reasons for Wanting to Lose Weight:

1) _____

_____

2) _____

_____

3) _____

_____

4) _____

_____

5) _____

_____

6) _____

_____

7 _____

_____

8) _____

_____

9) _____

_____

10) _____

_____

4) The fourth thing I did in planning to get started was to pick a starting date. I chose a Monday (the best day, I believe, to start something new)—a Monday about three weeks away. The approximate three-week period gave me time to do some important preparation:

a) I gradually reduced my consumption of sugar, salt, and caffeine. Like almost all Americans, I was addicted to them. I used them in great quantities (particularly salt), and I knew they were not at all good for me. I switched to decaffeinated coffee and tea (gradually, not all at once). I also stopped drinking soft drinks containing caffeine. By the end of the three-week period, I had eliminated sugar and caffeine, and greatly reduced my salt intake. *Just doing that made me feel much better.* Also, I was amazed at how much better my food tasted without being covered with salt.

b) I finished the task I started at the Valentine's Day weekend retreat: climbing out on that limb and sawing it off behind me. I announced to my family and a few friends that they would soon begin to see a difference in me, that I was going to lose weight and "that's that, I've made up my mind; it's going to happen, watch and see!"

I wasn't bragging at all. I was just determined. My reasons for wanting to lose weight were good and I was motivated to accomplish my goals. My starting date was coming up and I was ready! *"Fat, beware . . . you're gonna have to come off!!"*

Did the thought of failure ever enter my mind during this process? Of course, not only then but prior to then and since then, but I didn't let it stop me. If you don't take risks, you'll never accomplish anything worthwhile. I heard that Teddy Roosevelt once said, "It's far better to strive to accomplish great things and even fail than to live in that middle ground—that never, never land where one knows neither success nor failure."

You won't fail. Follow the plan outlined in this book and you will succeed in becoming that slimmer, healthier person you want to be. It's working for me, and prior to this I had been an absolute flop in the area of weight control.

c) And, finally, during the three weeks leading up to my starting date, I was preparing myself emotionally and mentally. I looked forward to that date. I became excited at the prospects of defeating this problem . . . there was now hope that I would win; it was like a light shining brightly at the end of a dark tunnel. The relatively small accomplishments during these three weeks gave me confidence that tremendous success was just around the corner! You, too, will come to know that hope and confidence.

Pick your starting date. Get out your calendar and pick a Monday approximately three weeks from now to start. You have to not only be motivated, *but you have to start!* Just picking the starting date will even further motivate you. It's exciting to begin to move from theory to practical application.

Write in your starting date below:

My starting date is Monday _____

(DATE)

Congratulations! Now begin immediately to gradually reduce your consumption of sugar, salt and caffeine. Also, crawl out on that limb and saw it off behind you (tell others they will begin to see the results soon). Prepare yourself emotionally and mentally, looking forward to your starting date. *I'm excited for you. You've started a journey that will result in a new you!*

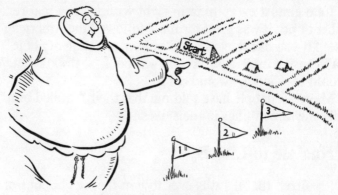

That's my starting date.

3

The Start . . . Bringing Your Body under Control

The Spoiled Brat

I had known for a long time that my body was a "spoiled brat" wanting to be pampered and fed all the goodies it could hold. Like almost all Americans, I never was *really hungry* when I ate; I ate because I enjoyed it, I ate on impulse, I ate to relieve stress, frustrations, etc., etc. I would even plan my daily activities to include the maximum number of eating opportunities. Do you ever do this?

I ate almost everything in sight without any real regard to whether or not it was good for me. I followed the American Food Motto: "If you like it, eat it, and be sure to eat plenty of it." I was like a friend of mine who said he was on a "seafood" diet. When he would *see* food, he would eat it!

Many fat people have told me that their "spoiled brat" does exactly the same things in their lives.

A Principle to Live By

I realized that if I was ever to win the weight control war I had been in practically all my life, I would have to be in control of my body. No longer could my body dictate my life style, tell me what to do and eat—I would have to be in charge of my life, and my body would have to be subject to me instead of the other way around (the way it had been for years).

You and I—in fact all people—know that the real person, the basic person, the essence of a person is not the flesh, blood and bones we see in the mirror but the inner person we cannot see with our eyes. Paul the Apostle, in his writings, referred to this as the "inner man." This "inner man" is also called "the spirit of man" and "that part of man which is created in the image of God." This "real you" is who needs to be in *control* . . . not your body . . . not the "spoiled brat." You be in control!

Therefore, not only *must you be* in control of your life, *you can be!* No longer will your body control you and dictate your life style; you will be in control of your body. Exciting? You bet it is! You are on your way to winning!

Use what I call the "U.B.I.C. Principle": *You Be In Control.* This principle will be a friendly, daily reminder that you're in control, *that you're the boss over your body.* The last few pages of this book are small posters entitled *"Remember the U.B.I.C. Principle." Cut them out and put one poster on your refrigerator*

An exciting idea was born in my life!

door and the other on the dash of your car (a little piece of tape will hold it). And you can also make hand-drawn copies or machine copies of the posters to put in other places.

A Brief Review

Before you move to the next chapter, let's review for a moment where you've come to now in this process of winning:

1) You've honestly faced up to the fact that you're fat, *and* you want to change that.

2) You've set your goal . . . for both the number of pounds you want to lose and the number of months in which you wish to lose them.

3) You've also listed your reasons for wanting to lose weight . . . that's your motivation spelled out in black and white right in front of you.

4) You've picked a starting date approximately three weeks away.

5) And you're now in the process of using the three weeks for the personal preparation described toward the end of chapter 2 (You're gradually reducing your intake of salt, sugar and caffeine, etc.)

6) You've also put up your U.B.I.C. posters.

You're right on target . . . congratulations!!!

Remember . . . Remember!

The preparation to lose weight (psychologically, physically, emotionally, spiritually, etc.) is *at least as important* as the actual day-by-day program itself. Therefore, be sure to do what chapters 1, 2 and 3 tell you to do *before* you do what chapter 4 tells you to do. Otherwise, you will not get the best results.

When our sons were small I purchased a toy fire truck, one of the large assemble-it-yourself deals. Assuming I knew how to do it, I plunged right in hooking things together and so on. Several hours later I wised up, read the instructions, followed them step by step, and discovered (much to my delight) how quickly the fire truck came together. The old adage, "When all else fails, read the instructions," proved to be wisdom.

Follow the instructions . . . right down to putting up your U.B.I.C. posters. With the proper preparation, you will be very excited about the results. *You can do it!* In fact, U.B.I.C. can also stand for "You Bet I Can!"

4

Beginning
Your New Life Style

Getting Initial Control

Now the starting date is here. It's time to bring your body under control. The body must *first be brought under control;* then control can be maintained. It's also time to weigh yourself, and, if you wish, take measurements—"vital statistics." Near the back of the book you will find a personal progress chart where you should record the results. You should weigh yourself once per week—at the same time of day, on the same scales and wearing the same clothes. Take measurements only once each thirty days.

I decided upon a simple plan to bring my body under control. I got the idea for the plan from the Old Testament story of Daniel the prophet. In chapter one of the Book of Daniel, he requested that he and his friends not be required to eat the rich food and wine normally given to the king's servants, but that they be fed only "pulse and water" for ten days. Then a visual comparison would be made between Daniel's group and the other servants. At the end of the ten-day period Daniel and his friends looked "healthier and better nourished."

Daniel and his friends only ate "pulse" and drank water for ten days. While the word "pulse" is usually translated "vegetables," some scholars believe that fruits would also have been included. So for ten days I would only drink water and eat only those things I knew would be good for me: vegetables and fruits.

If it's good enough for Daniel . . .

Like Daniel, I should also be healthier after the ten days. Very important too is that after the ten days I would be in control of my body . . . *I would now be in charge.* My body would now be subject to me. This is the way it should have been all along.

Here's what I ate during the ten days:

1) Fresh fruits of all types (oranges, apples, grapefruit, peaches, grapes, etc.)

2) Unsweetened fruit juices of all types. Also, vegetable juices are excellent if they are not loaded down with salt.

3) Fresh vegetables of all sorts (including melons). I particularly like cantaloupes and watermelons.

4) Dried fruits, fruits canned in juice (not syrup), and vegetables canned in water.

Drink all the juice you want, and eat all the fruits and vegetables you want. I would drink several glasses of juice at a time. I would eat four or five very large navel oranges at a sitting, or eat more than a pound of pineapple. I would eat all the tomatoes, potatoes, onions, green beans or peas I could hold. I would eat them raw or cooked in water or steamed. For spices, I would use garlic powder, onion powder, black pepper and even a *little* salt.

During the ten days, your purpose is not to lose weight. Your purpose is to gain control over your body. And you're doing it by feeding your body the very things that will improve your body's health. It's a no-lose situation—gaining control and becoming healthier too! Another plus is that *you will also almost certainly lose weight* during the ten days. It's not the goal but an exciting additional result.

A Little Discomfort?

During the first two or three days, you may experience some slight discomfort—occasional headaches, queasiness, a bad taste in your mouth, or bad breath. Your body, having been accustomed to getting whatever it wanted, rebels. It reacts to the change in diet. Also, depending on how effectively you eased off caffeine, sugar and salt during the three weeks prior to your starting date, the discomfort you experience could be in large part withdrawal symptoms. Breaking any addiction can be painful and uncomfortable. Also, I'm told that with only pure foods being consumed, the body begins to clean itself up. This too can contribute to some slight discomfort for a brief time.

You can minimize the discomfort by drinking lots and lots of water. Water flushes your system; it helps to rid the body of toxic wastes. Your body, of course, consists of a very high percentage of water; the body needs a lot of water to operate at peak efficiency. In addition to drinking a lot of juice during the first ten days, I drank several large glasses of water each day.

Do not be discouraged. The discomfort (if you experience any, and you may be one who doesn't) quickly passes and then you begin to feel absolutely great! After two or three days I felt super physically. I was more alert and I had more energy than before. And even more important than that, I felt great about myself! I was now winning, I was now in charge, I was gaining control over my body. *The U.B.I.C. Principle was being applied to my life, and it was working!*

5

Day by Day . . . A New You Is on the Way

Remember . . . You're Not on a "Diet"

You have now completed the ten-day startup period during which you ate only vegetables and fruits and you drank only water and fruit juice. *Congratulations! You're off to a great start. You're certainly healthier, you've probably already lost weight, and you're now in control of your body.* You're in charge and on your way to a new you!

You're not dieting. You're assuming (taking) control of your life; you're establishing a new life style; you're setting up a new standard for daily living. Old habits are being broken and a new you is coming forth for the world to see! *That's exciting!*

Changes in Attitudes and Practices

You're in control, you've made real progress, you feel great about yourself, and going back to the old life style is out of the question. You now focus your energies and attitudes on the present and the future. Your new life style is under way and nothing can stop you! When I was at this point, I felt as though I could leap over a building or wrestle alligators with one arm tied behind my back. I still feel that way!

31

In establishing my new life style, I daily put into practice certain ideas (principles) that have worked extremely well:

1) Every day I remind myself that I am in control of my body, that I am in charge of my life: "Goodin, remember the U.B.I.C. Principle—*You Be In Control!*" I'm told it's OK to talk to yourself just as long as you don't answer.

2) I don't ever think in terms of calories when I'm eating. If I had to count calories, I would simply stay fat . . . I refuse to count them. I don't count them and I've lost a great deal of weight.

3) It's far more important *when* you eat than *how much* you eat. I eat one very large meal a day (usually at lunch but sometimes at breakfast), and one light meal (usually at breakfast but sometimes *early* evening). I usually don't eat in the evening except for a piece of fruit or a glass of juice. The average person (controlled by his body, habits, and circumstances) will eat a very large meal at night and then become a "couch potato" . . . and *fat piles on.*

I probably eat as much now as I have ever eaten. I simply eat at different times (*by my choice*) and make some different food choices, and it's working great. I don't feel at all deprived. I'm not hungry, and I feel great about myself . . . no longer does my body control me! That's fantastic!

4) It's far more important *what you eat than how much* you eat. As my grandpa Jordan use to say, "I've decided to use the common sense that the good Lord gave me." That common sense led me to these conclusions and practices:

a) I was already eating lots of fruits and vegetables, so I continued to do that. What could be better for you than that? I ate all I wanted except I would only have a snack in the evening. To get even more fiber (with little or no fat), I would continue to eat lots of beans and rice (usually for a main meal).

b) I was already drinking lots of water and unsweetened fruit juice, so I continued to do that. Since I had already stopped drinking caffeine-laced beverages, I simply continued the same way. It's amazing how much better you feel simply by leaving off caffeine.

c) I had drastically reduced my consumption of refined sugar and salt, so I continued to do that. Doctors and other health/nutrition professionals agree that these are definitely not good for you. I believe they are also addictive. *I'm in control of my life;* I don't want anything to control me ever again. Incidentally, there is usually enough naturally occurring sugar and sodium in foods to meet your body's requirements.

d) I enjoy meat, so I continued to eat meat; however, I decided to avoid eating fat as much as possible. I read recently that "the fat you eat is the fat you wear." I eat trimmed and lean beef and pork in moderation, and I eat skinned poultry and a variety of seafood. I eat meat with my large meal, and I usually avoid fried varieties unless the meat can be fried without grease. To further avoid fat, I very sparingly use items such as butter, margarine, mayonnaise, etc.

America's four basic food groups are caffeine, sugar, salt, and grease. I decided (my choice . . . remember the U.B.I.C. Principle) to no longer follow that crowd. These "food groups"

America's four "basic" food groups:

Sugar

Grease

Caffeine

Salt

are clearly seen at normal meal times, but perhaps even more clearly at snack time: soft drinks, potato chips, candy bars, etc. As snacks, I've decided instead to enjoy fruits, fruit juice, melons, etc. Nothing is better than a slice of watermelon or half a cantaloupe as a snack. "Eat the wrong snacks, let out your slacks."

e) I occasionally enjoy desserts—not every day and usually with my large meal. Common sense told me that this should be done in moderation. And if I can have a dessert sweetened with an artificial sweetener, I choose that. Remember, the U.B.I.C. Principle allows you to say "yes" and it allows you to say "no." *Isn't it great to have that freedom, to be in charge, never again to be controlled by sweets or anything else?*

Some Exciting Food Choices

Since you are not "dieting" but establishing a new life style (a new "normal"), you can enjoy a wide variety of exciting foods. I sure do. I enjoy eating and losing weight too! That's motivating.

Some of the exciting foods I enjoy (and eat lots of) are:

1) *Honey* is a great natural sweetener. I use delicious honey as a topping (and sweetener) for cold and hot cereals. Fix oatmeal or Cream of Wheat (piping hot), pour honey on top and add a

"How sweet it is"

little milk. What a great breakfast! And honey does great things for a bowl of corn flakes or raisin bran. Also, honey is great to add just a touch of sweetness to cooked vegetables such as corn, green peas, and green beans. Honey makes a great dessert too. Put honey on a slice of homemade bread. What a great way to end a meal!

I'm told that honey is nature's perfect food; it's the only food that will not spoil, wither, or in some fashion decay even when not refrigerated. I read about a container of honey being found when an ancient Egyptian tomb was opened for the first time. It apparently had been left for the dead man to use in the next life. The Egyptians would often bury whole boats, even slaves, with the deceased for him to use in the next world. The honey, thousands of years old, was still fresh and delicious.

My grandmother used to give me a tablespoon full of honey to soothe a sore throat. It worked! A doctor once told me that honey, being very acidic, will kill undesirable bacteria. You may also recall that honey made up a significant portion of John the Baptist's diet. It is an excellent natural food. Use it in good health.

2) *Peanuts* make a great meal all by themselves. As I said earlier, Daniel and his friends ate "pulse and water." "Pulse" can be literally rendered "leguminous plants." A leguminous plant is one that grows from a seed and that yields a pod. Examples are green bean plants or green pea plants—or *peanuts.* Eaten raw or roasted (no oil or salt), peanuts are both delicious and good for you. Often I will use a few ounces of peanuts as part of my light meal. Though peanuts do contain fat, it is not the artery-clogging, saturated kind of fat. Filling, delicious, and good for you . . . that's hard to beat! Will you still lose weight? Yes!

3) *Oriental food.* I can't use chopsticks, but I can sure make the food disappear. For my large meal, I often eat oriental food. I prefer Chinese and Korean food but I also like Japanese cooking. Simple oriental dishes are easy to fix at home, very nutritious (containing meat and vegetables), delicious, and so good for you. There are many packaged oriental foods in the grocery store, and many good cookbooks are readily available. The variety is

You thought these were forbidden, but they're not.

Oriental Food

Peanuts

"A little nuts"

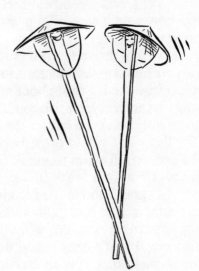

"Chop chop!"

High-fiber bread

Frozen yogurt

Pasta

practically endless (to suit any taste), relatively easy to prepare, and moderately priced. What a way to eat!

For my large meal, I occasionally go to a Chinese luncheon buffet and eat until I develop a strange urge to go home and plant rice in my yard. I thoroughly enjoy myself! And still lose weight? Yes! Remember, your new life style is not a "diet" but an approach to when and what to eat that allows you to enjoy delicious foods in abundance. *Remember the U.B.I.C. Principle!* It's great! It works!

Incidentally, I will occasionally take in a seafood buffet for my large meal, usually at lunch but once in a while in the early evening. I have been known to eat seafood until the ocean drops six inches. I eat only seafood and a little fruit if it's available; I leave off the other trimmings.

4) *Breads and pasta.* You thought these might be forbidden, but they are not. Foods high in fiber (whole wheat and rye breads) and foods high in complex carbohydrates (pasta) contain little fat, are very satisfying (filling), and a high percentage of their calories pass through your system undigested.

Concerning the place of bread in weight loss, I read in the *Reader's Digest* (Nov. '87) of a group of overweight young men who were dieting. In addition to whatever else they ate, they were told to eat twelve slices of bread a day. Some ate ordinary white bread and some ate high-fiber bread. After eight weeks, the men who ate the ordinary white bread had lost an average 13.7 pounds, while those who ate high-fiber bread had lost an average of 19.4 pounds—more than 40 percent greater weight loss.

A lady in our church recently baked for me a loaf of high-fiber homemade bread. She brought it on a Sunday morning and I ate it for lunch. I ate the whole thing for my large meal that day. I also drank lots of water. Filling, delicious, nutritious, *and* helpful in losing weight. What a great way to lose weight . . . much better than cottage cheese and lettuce leaves, *wouldn't you agree?*

How about a heaping plate of spaghetti smothered with a thick sauce made with tomato paste, green peppers, onions, tomato pieces, and mushrooms? Sounds delicious! You know it is! And lose weight too? Yes. Eat it early (for your large meal) and enjoy! How about beef or sausage in the sauce? Use just a little, or, better yet, leave it out. You really won't miss it all that much and you'll avoid all that animal fat. An excellent option is to use turkey or chicken chunks as the meat in the sauce. They are low in fat and delicious.

5) *Frozen yogurt.* It's at least as good as ice cream. Frozen yogurt outlets have become very popular in the past few years, for very good reasons. Frozen yogurt tastes as good as fine ice cream, is very nutritious, and is lower in fat and calories than ice cream. It's usually less expensive too. By the way, many people who don't particularly like dairy-case yogurt love frozen yogurt.

One of my favorite frozen yogurt dishes consists of a warm Belgian waffle covered with a generous portion of French vanilla frozen yogurt. This is topped off with your choice of three fresh fruit toppings (with juice) and low-calorie whipped cream. Filling, nutritious, delicious, and even low in calories (fewer than 400), this "lite" Belgian waffle makes a great meal.

6

And a Little Pain Too

The "Couch Potato" Generation

Although most people are busy, even very busy, few choose to exercise. We have become a generation of spectators, sitting and watching others exercise (sports on TV, etc.). A typical evening goes something like this: eat a big dinner (the wrong time to eat a big meal and often the wrong types of food), then sit down for the evening (the wrong thing to do) *and the fat piles on.* We try to justify our actions by saying that we've worked all day and need our nourishment and rest. Many people "justify" themselves to an early grave. It's a shame. They could live longer and enjoy life much more if they would simply make a few wise choices about what (and when) to eat, and exercise. The "couch potato" generation can become the "be healthier, live longer, and enjoy life more" generation.

You've Chosen a Different Life Style

You've decided to follow a different drummer. You're establishing a new life style, a new "normal." You're making intelligent choices about when to eat and what to eat. You're on your way to a healthier, slimmer new you!

Another choice you now need to make is the choice to exercise regularly—moderately at first and more vigorously later. In one study, doctors followed the progress of 300 fat people who had each lost 70 or more pounds and kept it off. There were two things that all 300 had in common: they reduced the amount of fat they were eating, and they had all increased their physical activity. Exercise kicks your metabolism into high gear so that you burn up fat at top speed while preserving your muscle or lean tissue.

Walking: The Perfect Exercise

At one time, of course, walking was the world's most popular (and only) mass-transit system. If you wanted to go somewhere, you walked—or you didn't go. Interestingly, today, in the midst of our high technology and numerous alternative means of transportation, walking is once again becoming very popular, this time as a means of improving our health.

A regular program of walking will help you lose weight, help tone your flabby muscles, help prevent heart disease, and help alleviate stress and depression. In fact, some people even believe that walking helps reverse some of the physical aspects of aging. One very early, very noticeable effect of walking is an improved sense of well-being—physical and mental.

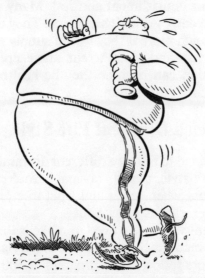

Makes you feel better than good!

Walking may very well be the perfect form of exercise. It doesn't stress the body the way running does, and it's something that everyone can do. Swimming is great but you have to have a pool. If you want to purchase home exercise equipment or join a quality health spa, that's great; you'll benefit from the workouts. But walking costs nothing and can be done almost anywhere.

Start your daily walking program slowly. You don't want to overdo it; in fact, if it's been a long while since you've had a physical checkup, it would be a good idea to do that before you start. Once you've got the go-ahead, pick a good pair of walking shoes (good arch support and cushioned soles are important) and decide on your walking course. Always walk where it's safe. Stay away from traffic—walkers and cars don't mix well. I carry with me either a walking stick or a long, folded umbrella. It gives me something to do with my hands and it's a great tool to discourage overly curious dogs.

Start off slowly, particularly if you're in poor physical condition, gradually building up to as fast a pace as you can handle. It's best to walk daily, but walk at least thirty minutes a day, three or four days a week. In inclement weather you can walk in a shopping mall or in a gym. Walking alone provides a great opportunity for thinking, reflecting on the day's activities, planning, praying, etc. Walking with someone provides great fellowship and an opportunity for some stimulating conversation. Walking is fun!

7

What to Do
When You Mess Up

We All Do It!

Early one Thursday evening I went to a restaurant for a business meeting. The meeting was designed so that the participants could arrive to eat any time between six and seven-thirty P.M. . . . the business session would start promptly at eight. I arrived around six P.M. and ordered "all you can eat" shrimp. That was a pretty good choice: this was my big meal for the day, I had eaten only some fruit and a small salad earlier in the day, and I had planned to eat only shrimp (leaving off the other trimmings) and a little fruit. It was a little late in the day for my big meal, but I had to attend the meeting so I planned my day accordingly.

I ate shrimp until the alarm sounded that the ocean had dropped six inches. That's OK (remember, I don't count calories). What you eat and when you eat are much more important than how much you eat. I finished off the meal with some fruit and moved on into the business session. When the meeting was over, I had a craving for hot fudge cake and a cup of coffee . . . *I could almost taste that vanilla ice cream surrounded by chocolate cake and covered with hot fudge.* Ordinarily I would think to myself, "Goodin, remember the U.B.I.C. Principle. You Be In Control!!" I would simply say "no" to the craving and go on home, perhaps eating a piece of fruit when I got there.

But I gave in. I ate the hot fudge cake, drank my coffee and

42

Gotcha!

enjoyed the dickens out of it. And that's not all! On the way home, I stopped at a Mexican food outlet and ate four or five tacos and drank a huge thirty-two-ounce cup of cola. *And even that's not all.* Just before I got home I stopped at a convenience store, drank a pint of chocolate milk and ate a jelly roll cake. I had blown it *big time* . . . in fact, when I got home, *I still ate the fruit.*

It's How You Handle It That Counts

I was very much like the backslidden fat person shown in the illustration above. I had blown it royally; I felt like the little boy caught with six cookies in his left hand and his right hand down in the cookie jar. I was absolutely guilty and there was no denying it.

At that point I was at a crossroads, I had a choice to make: I could say, "To the dickens with it all!" and return to my old out-of-control life style where my body ruled me, *or* I could keep things in perspective and realize that messing up from time to time is a part of living, that it was only a momentary distraction in my new life style. I chose, of course, to keep things in proper perspective; I was in this thing for the long haul . . . I didn't get as fat as I was overnight and I would not lose the weight overnight. Messing up didn't change a thing in the long run; when Friday morning came, I was back on my way to becoming the new me . . . back in control, the way it should be.

Don't Ever Give Up!

Life is not always fair; it can at times subject us to enormous pressures and stress. We sometimes respond by eating food like it won't be available after today. People find comfort and momentary escape in eating. Thus, depending on what's going on in your life, "backsliding" can also be for a much longer period of time than just the momentary "mess up" described earlier.

After making tremendous progress in my weight loss program (I had lost well over 100 pounds at the time), I experienced a period of backsliding that lasted several months. My father was seriously ill for a time and he then died. Also, in our church, we were experiencing some real challenges. For a time, those difficult circumstances seemed to short circuit my motivation to lose weight . . . I gained about 25 pounds. Gradually, however, I began to get back under control. I began to reapply the U.B.I.C. Principle, I lost the weight I had gained, and I am continuing to lose.

I didn't give up—*AND DON'T YOU GIVE UP!!* You fail only when you quit trying. You can always come back from any point of backsliding.

Divide . . . and Win!

While a succesful weight loss program involves goals accomplished over months and even years, the immediate battlefront is always today . . . how to make it successfully today is the immediate issue. While some days the battle is relatively easy, other days can be very tough.

To help win the daily battle on those difficult days, I use the technique I call, "Divide and Win." It works like this:

1. Divide your waking hours into three-hour segments—for example, 6 to 9 A.M., 9 A.M. to noon, noon to 3 P.M., 3 to 6 P.M., 6 to 9 P.M., and 9 P.M. to midnight.

2. As you begin each three-hour segment, ask yourself two questions:

- What shall I do and/or eat during these three hours that will contribute to the success of my weight loss program?
- What should I avoid doing or eating during these same three hours?

Answer the questions honestly and follow your own good advice.

3. Remind yourself that victory on that particular day will be won three hours at a time. Before you know it, a successful day has passed.

When you use the "Divide and Win" technique, you're in effect applying the U.B.I.C. Principle in small segments. Some days it just seems more manageable to do it that way.

You're doing great! Whatever the challenge may be, you're on the way to greater victories. *You are winning! Congratulations!*

8

A Typical Week with "Dr. John"

Congratulations!

You're making tremendous progress:

1) You've set your weight-loss goal—both the number of pounds you want to lose and the number of months in which you want to lose them.

2) You've listed your reasons for wanting to lose weight . . . your motivation is right in front of you, spelled out in black and white. You've also put up your U.B.I.C. Principle posters.

3) You picked your starting date and did the personal preparation during the three weeks leading up to your starting date.

4) Beginning with your starting date, you completed the ten-day period during which you brought your body under control.

5) And now you're in a daily routine of developing a new "normal," a new life style. The new you is on the way. You may have even messed up a time or two and handled the situation just fine.

Every Week Is Different

No two weeks are the same; I thought, however, it could be helpful for you to see how I would spend a typical week. By the

46

way, "Dr. John" is a nickname or term of affection someone hung on me years ago and it stuck. It probably came about because "Rev. Goodin" or "Dr. Goodin" seemed too formal and just plain "John" seemed a bit too informal. So "Dr. John" seemed to fit just right.

A Typical Week:

Sunday

Breakfast—In the early A.M., I have a large glass of juice and/or half a cantaloupe.

Lunch—When we get home from church (around 1 P.M.), I eat whatever Shelba fixes for Sunday dinner—meatloaf, spaghetti, Swedish meatballs, etc. She includes lots of vegetables or salad and usually some type of high-fiber bread. I go kind of light on my meat and eat lots of everything else. Instead of salt I use lots of pepper, garlic and onion powder, and I experiment with various herbs and spices. I occasionally use a little salt on fresh vegetables, particularly sliced onion.

Dinner—Around 5 or 6 o'clock, I have a sixteen-ounce can of fruit cocktail (canned in juice without sugar) or a twenty-ounce can of pineapple chunks (canned in their own juice without sugar), or a piece of fresh fruit or two . . . or a slice of melon.

I drink my water with my meals, and for an afternoon snack I might have a piece of fruit or a few ounces of raw or roasted peanuts.

I rarely exercise on Sunday.

Monday

Breakfast—In the early A.M., I have a whole-wheat English muffin (toasted) with honey and a cup of decaf coffee.

Lunch—I have a small salad w/fruit and water.

Dinner—In the early P.M. I eat approximately one-half pound of roasted peanuts and some fruit, and I drink water.

I walk approximately two miles.

Tuesday

Breakfast—In the A.M. I drink fruit juice and a glass of water, and eat a small bowl of high-fiber cereal.

Lunch—I enjoy a Chinese buffet at a restaurant, drinking water and eating until China complains to the U.N.

Dinner—In the early P.M. I eat fresh fruit or a slice of watermelon.

I walk approximately two miles.

Wednesday

Breakfast—In the A.M., I have fruit juice, two eggs, whole-wheat toast and decaf coffee, along with a glass of water.

Lunch—I eat fresh fruit and/or a raw vegetable salad and have water to drink.

Dinner—In the early P.M. I have frozen yogurt on a Belgian waffle with fresh fruit toppings, and water to drink.

For a snack, I have a piece of fruit or half a cantaloupe.

Thursday

Breakfast—In the early A.M. I have fruit juice and a glass of water, and perhaps a whole-wheat English muffin.

Lunch—I have a bowl of soup, high-fiber bread, and water to drink, or I may skip lunch depending on what Shelba may be planning for dinner.

Dinner—In the early P.M., Shelba prepares a Korean rice dish containing vegetables and lean meat. I eat lots of this with water to drink.

I walk approximately two miles.

Friday

Breakfast—In the early A.M., I have fruit juice and a glass of water, and perhaps a piece of fresh fruit.

Lunch—I enjoy a salad bar that includes pasta and fruits. The pasta is hot and I top it with meatless tomato sauce and a little parmesan cheese. I drink water and I eat lots, but I go easy on salad dressings.

Dinner—In the early P.M. I eat fresh or canned fruit, or perhaps a melon portion.

Usually one day each week I go to a local health spa I joined a number of years ago. I have a lifetime membership. I do some stretching exercises and use an exercise bicycle—no heavy weights, etc.

Saturday

Breakfast—Shelba fixes something special for Saturday breakfast . . . French toast, Cream of Wheat (great with honey and milk), or pancakes. I try to use reasonable control. I drink water and a cup of decaf coffee.

Lunch—In early to mid afternoon, Shelba and I go shopping and we usually eat out. I get a salad bar or a sandwich of turkey or fish. I drink water.

Dinner—I have a snack of fruit or a slice of melon.

I usually go to bed early on Saturday night, but first I walk approximately two miles.

Just remember that the basic idea is to eat one large meal and one small meal per day, to eat them early (usually) and then have a snack for dinner or an early dinner if dinner is to be a meal. Between-meal snacks should be fruit, fruit juice, melon or raw vegetables. By the way, you should avoid casserole dishes unless you know exactly what's in them; though delicious, they are often loaded with high-fat items such as butter or sour cream, etc. You can certainly make your own casseroles and make them healthy and delicious. And, of course, the moderate exercise program should become part of your daily life style.

Following the basic principles outlined in this book, you can enjoy a wide variety of delicious foods. You will not go around hungry nor will you feel deprived. In fact, you will feel the best you've ever felt in your life. You will become slimmer and healthier and enjoy the trip getting there.

9

A Word to the Spouse and Family

My wife and sons were very concerned about my being so fat; they, of course, didn't want me to die prematurely. Fat people's lives are often shortened because of the many problems related to obesity: heart disease, kidney disease, high blood pressure, diabetes, stroke, etc. Medical science has also shown that, with proper weight control, many of these problems lessen or disappear. Some damage may even begin to reverse itself, and the body begins to heal.

With the very best of intentions, family members will try to change the fat person's life style by calling to his attention his overeating and/or his eating the wrong things. It's as if the family members hope to effect a positive change in the person by criticizing his problems. This does not work, in fact, it works to quite the opposite result: the fat person often becomes angry and resentful, and eats even more. His behavior is not very reasonable, but I know from experience that's often how fat people respond. It's much like the experience of the man who stepped on a honeybee and was stung. He said, "I'll show you," and he went and sat down on a hornet's nest. He, by his response, made his problem worse rather than better.

The spouse and other family members need to be positive and encouraging in relating to the obese person. Say something like "Honey (Dad), I know that you could become slimmer and healthier if you just decided to; you can do anything you put your mind to." The fat person knows he has a problem, and he doesn't mind the family's concern (in fact, he even appreciates it) provided that concern is not expressed in criticism.

Following my Valentine's Day weekend mini-sermon in which I challenged myself and those present to get our bodies under control, to win victory over our weight problems, my wife, Shelba, became very positive and supportive. In fact, she didn't say much except to encourage me. Shelba put it this way: "I decided to quit doing so much talking and to do more encouraging and praying." It's working. My whole family is now very supportive; they are just as excited about the victory I'm winning as I am. Also, members of our church family have been tremendously encouraging and supportive. As I keep them posted on my progress, they will often spontaneously break into applause. As a friend back home used to say, "Makes me feel plum good all over!"

If more than one family member needs to lose weight, the two can be of great encouragement and support to each other. Someone once defined fellowship as "two fellows in the same ship." Fat family members are in the same ship and can be of real help to each other.

A Word from Shelba

Hi, I'm "Dr. John's" wife taking the opportunity to "get in the last word." Just kidding, of course, but I too want to share a few thoughts with you:

1) I'd cook John huge meals, he would brag on my cooking while he was eating lots of it, and then I would fuss at him for eating so much.

2) When we ate out (at a restaurant or at a friend's home) John would embarrass me by how much he ate. I would feel like crawling under the table and hiding. "Don't you think you've had enough!" I nagged and nagged.

3) I didn't want him to die on me. I loved him and wanted to change him but he just seemed to eat more and more. His breathing got heavier, his snoring got louder, his walking got slower, and

he continually outgrew his clothes. Our sons were also concerned; they would often comment to me about their Dad's need to lose weight. They would even occasionally speak to John but without success. The efforts would almost always backfire.

4) Finally, I quit trying to force a change. I began to encourage him and I began to pray daily for him. I earnestly began to ask the Lord to do what I couldn't do—help John to adopt a healthier life style. It worked! After several months, John planned and began the program described in this book—*and it's working!*

5) I'm so proud of John; I've taken up most of his pants, he has purchased smaller shirts, *and he looks great!* I would even marry him all over again. The future looks bright for a slimmer, healthier "Dr. John"; we're looking forward to the future together.

6) I encourage you to apply the principles of this book to your own life. You'll be glad you did. Also, give a copy to a friend. He'll be glad you did.

Attaboy!

10

Important Questions and Answers

Q. Will the "buddy system" help me in this program?
A. Yes . . . it's always helpful to do something with a friend. You can encourage, support and pray for each other. You can rejoice in the victories together, and you can encourage each other in the difficult times. You can walk together; some great conversations take place while walking from here to yonder and back. You each should have your own copy of this book to write down your goals, motivation and progress.

The program also works great on your own. Some people prefer it that way. I did not have a "buddy" and I'm doing just great!

Q. How important is fiber in my daily diet?
A. Very, very important. The vast majority of health and nutrition professionals agree that a daily food intake of high fiber and low fat is the healthiest way to go. High-fiber foods such as whole-grain cereals and breads, vegetables and fruits greatly benefit the body; they help you to be regular, they cleanse the body, *and* (in a delicious, satisfying fashion) they fill you *up* without filling you *out*. Also, there are many who believe that there's a direct correlation between a high-fiber diet and reduced instances of cancer. The program you and I are following embraces this very healthy approach to daily living. Be healthier, be slimmer, and feel better too . . . that's even better than exciting!

Q. I'm doing so well on the program—can I ever have a "reward" . . . something I might not normally eat?

A. Yes . . . remember the U.B.I.C. Principle—You Be In Control. Using good, common sense, you simply make that choice. Every once in a while, I'll get a large "Cherries Jubilee" milk shake and enjoy every sip. I don't do it often, but when I do, I enjoy it and then it's behind me. And when I do have a "reward," I'll often make some adjustments, maybe substituting it for the small meal, or leaving off other snacks that day. The great thing about being in control of your life is that you have the freedom to make choices; you're not in bondage to your body, neither are you in bondage to some "diet." You and I are not on a diet and never will be. We're in control; we, not our bodies, call the shots. That's fantastic! Now that also means that some days you may choose to have only fruits and fruit juices . . . maybe you got a little off track and need to come back on track.

Q. I'm weighing myself once a week like I'm supposed to, and I seem to have reached a plateau . . . is that normal?

A. Yes, that is normal . . . don't be concerned; just continue with your new life style and you'll break through the plateau. If the plateau seems to be particularly stubborn, there are some things you can do to quickly break through:

(1) For a week, each day eat your large meal at breakfast and your small meal at lunch.

(2) Add a half mile or a mile to your daily walking distance. Or if you're using another type of exercise, simply increase it slightly.

(3) Or, for a few days (perhaps a week) choose to eat only vegetables and fruits (all you want) and drink water and fruit juices. You'll be repeating for a few days what you did during the ten-day period when you first began the program. You're also renewing the control you have over your body; you'll feel great, and the plateau doesn't have a chance.

(4) Or, for a few days, you may choose to fast . . . that will quickly blow a plateau away. It's very healthy, and it's not nearly

as difficult as you may have thought. You simply leave off food, and drink lots of water (you can also include some juice if you feel you need to). Your body is already under control, so the adjustment to a brief fast is not difficult. During a fast your body further cleanses itself and heals itself; the energy the body normally uses in the digestive process is now turned inward toward repairing the body, giving it a chance to rest. When you end the fast, eat very light for a day or two; it helps the body to adjust back to your normal life style.

A brief fast from time to time will be a positive, healthy part of your new life style. In addition to the health benefits, there are also tremendous spiritual benefits to fasting. If you would like additional information about fasting, I recommend two books to you: *Fast Your Way to Health* by J. Harold Smith and *God's Chosen Fast* by Arthur Wallis.

Q. Should I take vitamins?

A. As you probably know, not all health and nutrition professionals agree on this issue, but I believe that you should take vitamins. With all the environmental pollution around us, with so many processed foods available to us, and with the use of chemical insecticides and chemical fertilizers in raising our crops, many people believe that it's difficult for our bodies to receive and maintain proper vitamin levels.

I daily take a good basic multivitamin/multimineral product. I also take Vitamin C. I buy them at a variety of places . . . drug stores, variety stores, nutrition stores, etc. The daily cost is minimal and I always watch for sales to further keep the cost down. I feel better when I regularly take vitamins; I believe they are a sound investment in your health.

Q. What about maintenance . . . once I reach my goal, how do I maintain my weight at the proper level?

A. It's very simple; you don't have to do anything new or different to maintain your weight. Remember what you've done . . . you have established a new life style, a new "normal"; you have applied the U.B.I.C. Principle to your life—you are in control. So what you do is simply choose to make whatever minor adjustments are necessary . . . change the time of day for meals, slightly increase or decrease the quantity of food at a meal, adjust the frequency of snacks, etc. Always remember that you're not on a diet; you've established a new life style . . . you don't have an old "normal" to go back to, thus maintenance is easy.

Excited about it!!

11

Valentine's Day Weekend Retreat Revisited

A Sweet Return

Back in chapter 1 I described the Valentine's Day weekend retreat when I challenged all the fat people (including myself) to get their lives under control, to win victory over their weight problems. What an exciting experience it was to return a year later, over a hundred pounds slimmer, and with an opportunity to share the victory with the people present. They rejoiced with me in the exciting progress I had made; in fact, a number of them had accepted my challenge of a year ago. One lady had lost over eighty pounds, another, forty pounds, and several men and women had lost twenty or more pounds.

I brought with me to this second retreat the sportscoat, pants and belt I had worn to the retreat a year earlier. To dramatize my weight loss, I modeled the clothes for the group. A year earlier I'd had to grunt, strain, and suck in my gut just to get the clothes on. Now the clothes were much too large even when worn over my present clothes. They literally swallowed me whole. A sweet return indeed!

Half the Man Really Becomes
Twice the Man

When I reach my ultimate weight loss goal, I will almost literally be half the man I used to be. You too are on your way to reach your weight loss goal. When you reach it, you may *physically* be half, or two thirds, or three fourths the man (or woman) you used to be; *but* in other ways . . . more important ways:

discipline	self-control	self-esteem
confidence	assurance	health

you'll be *twice* the man you used to be!

Two Keys to Continuing Success

If you have adopted the principles of this book, if you have applied them to your life, then you're on your way to a slimmer, healthier you. You've gained control over your body and you're establishing a new life style. You've quit dieting, and you've established a new "normal" mode for living.

There are two very important keys to your continuing success:

1) *Perseverance*

Perseverance is that quality known as stickability or determination to continue on a course of action. Adopt a long-range or lifetime view of this program and your success will in large part be assured. The "long haul" mentality will enable you to persevere. You'll be able to move forward *overcoming* every obstacle and setback.

2) *Flexibility*

A great basketball player will make whatever adjustments are necessary in order for him to make the greatest contribution to his team's success. The adjustments are usually not dramatic, but are the smaller, subtle adjustments *made in a timely fashion.* You'll need to do the same thing in this program. You'll need to make adjustments based on the level of your success. From time to time you'll need to make adjustments concerning what you eat, how much you eat, when you eat, how much you exercise, etc. The adjustments will not need to be dramatic, but smaller adjustments made when you need to make them. Just use that good common sense my grandpa Jordan used to talk about and you'll do just fine.

Persevere and *be flexible,* and your success will continue. Who knows, you may one day become known as the Magic Johnson or Larry Bird of weight control.

Best wishes, and may the Lord bless you real good.

Half the man equals twice the man!

12

Personal Progress Chart

Weigh-in Records

NOTE: Remember to weigh yourself once per week on the same day, at the same time of day. Use the same scale, and wear the same clothes.
You'll be excited at your progress!
Remember the U.B.I.C. Principle!

DATE	WEIGHT	DATE	WEIGHT	DATE	WEIGHT

Vital Statistics

(Measurements in inches)

DATE	WAIST	HIPS	BUST (CHEST)	THIGHS
____	____	____	____	____
____	____	____	____	____
____	____	____	____	____
____	____	____	____	____
____	____	____	____	____
____	____	____	____	____
____	____	____	____	____
____	____	____	____	____
____	____	____	____	____
____	____	____	____	____
____	____	____	____	____
____	____	____	____	____
____	____	____	____	____
____	____	____	____	____
____	____	____	____	____

13

Simple Recipes and Suggested Food Uses

The recipes in this chapter are not specifically "low calorie." They are designed to be recipes which are:

- Easy to prepare
- Delicious
- Relatively low in fat
- Relatively high in fiber

Of course, with any recipe, you can make it healthier with certain refinements:

1. Use low fat milk instead of whole milk.
2. Use "light" margarine instead of regular margarine.
3. Use "light" mayonnaise instead of regular mayonnaise.
4. Replace sour cream with yogurt.
5. Substitute honey for sugar (especially in baking).
6. Reduce sugar by 50 percent or more.
7. Reduce or omit salt.
8. Use your own creative ideas.

Can you enjoy good-tasting foods that are also good for you without going to a lot of extra work? Absolutely! Here are some of my favorite recipes. Not one of them is complicated, all of them are nutritious, and they taste great.

Many of them use honey, nature's perfect sweetener, which is also nutritious. It has calcium, potassium, phosphorous and vitamin C, plus traces of two B vitamins, copper and manganese—every one needed by the human body. Some suggestions for using it in food preparation are listed below, courtesy of the American Beekeeping Federation.

Honey Hints

Honey is a natural unrefined sweet made by honey bees from plant nectar.

Honey should be stored in a dry place. Because honey absorbs and retains moisture, refrigeration will hasten granulation.

Honey when granulated is not spoiled. It may be used granulated or reliquified. Place the honey container in a pan of warm water until the honey is clear.

Honey measures easily with a utensil that has been oiled or has been rinsed with hot water.

General Recipes

Easy Chicken Bake   Donna Dean[1]

1 box Stove Top Stuffing   1 can cream of chicken or
4 chicken breasts   cream of mushroom soup

1. Boil the chicken until it is tender; then remove the bones.
2. Prepare the stuffing according to the directions on the box but use only 1 cup of water and add the can of soup.
3. Pour half the stuffing into a casserole dish and top it with all of the chicken. Pour the remaining stuffing on top and bake it at 350° for 30 minutes or till it turns brown.

Chicken Pot Pie   Ida Dawson[1]

2 (9-inch) deep-dish pie shells   2 cups diced carrots
1 small hen   1 can chicken-mushroom soup
2 cups diced potatoes   1 can Le Sueur peas
   Use seasoning to your taste

1. Boil the hen and save the broth.
2. Cook the potatoes and carrots. Chop the meat into bite-size pieces. Mix the ingredients in a large bowl, adding broth as needed.
3. Pour the mixture into a pie shell, put the other shell on top, and bake the pie for 30 minutes at 325°.

Honey-Glazed Chicken   Bonnie Wilson[1]

¼ cup honey
3 tbsp. prepared mustard
1 tbsp. Worcestershire sauce
3 lbs. (12) chicken thighs
   or legs

shredded lettuce (optional)
spiced crab apples (optional)
2 tbsp. butter or margarine

1. In a small saucepan combine the honey, mustard, butter and Worcestershire sauce. Heat and stir the mixture until the butter melts.
2. Brush the chicken pieces with some of the honey mixture and arrange the chicken pieces skin side up in a large, shallow baking pan.
3. Bake the chicken uncovered for 45 to 50 minutes at 375° or until it is tender. Baste it with sauce once during baking.
4. Arrange the chicken pieces on a bed of shredded lettuce. Brush the remaining honey sauce over the chicken and garnish it with spiced crab apples.

Honey-Glazed Pork Chops   Pennie Jayne Reece[2]

½ cup wheat germ
1 tsp. paprika
¼ tsp. pepper
2 8 ½ oz. cans sliced pineapple
2 tbsp. lemon juice

⅓ cup flour
dash of salt
¼ cup honey
1 tbsp. prepared mustard
6 loin pork chops

1. Combine the wheat germ, flour, salt, paprika and pepper; then set them aside.

2. Add water to the pineapple syrup to make one cup of liquid. Add honey, lemon juice and mustard, mixing them well. Save the pineapple.

3. Brush both sides of the chops with the honey sauce. Dip the chops into the wheat germ mixture, turning them to coat them evenly.

4. Place the chops in a large, ungreased baking pan and bake them at 300° for 30 minutes or until they are well done. Garnish with pineapple.

Quick, Cheap (But Good) Soup (serves 8)   Bruce Chappell[1]

3 cans tomato soup   ½ bell pepper, diced
1 small onion, diced   1-lb. pkg. macaroni
   Use seasoning to your taste

1. Cook the macaroni according to the directions on the package, adding onion and bell pepper.

2. Drain the macaroni and add the tomato soup and 3 cans of water, mixing it thoroughly. Bring the soup to a boil, then reduce the heat and let it simmer for 20 minutes.

Garden Pea Casserole   Verna Phipps[1]

1 can garden peas, drained   ¾ cup bread crumbs
1 can mushroom soup   ¾ cup cheddar cheese, grated
1 small can water chestnuts

1. Mix the peas, soup and water chestnuts. Cover them with bread crumbs and cheese.

2. Bake the casserole at 350° until the crumbs and cheese are brown (about 30 minutes).

Squash Casserole   Shelba Goodin[1]

2 cups cooked squash, stewed   8 oz. sour cream
   with onions (drained)   1 pkg. Pepperidge Farm corn-
1 can cream of chicken soup   bread stuffing mix

1. Mix the soup, squash and sour cream together.
2. Put a layer of stuffing mix in the bottom of a baking dish. Pour in the other ingredients. Top the casserole with a layer of stuffing mix.
3. Bake it at 350° until it is brown and bubbly.

Green Bean Casserole (serves 4 to 6)   Carolyn Hare[1]

1 15-oz. can cut green beans;   1 can Durkee onion rings
  drain off one-half liquid   1 can cream of mushroom soup

Mix all the ingredients in a casserole dish and bake them at 375° for 45 minutes, uncovered for the last 5 or 10 minutes to brown.

Easy Baked Beans   Tony R. Gray[1]

1 large can pork and beans   bacon bits
½ cup molasses   minced onions
½ cup ketchup

1. Drain the pork and beans and mix them with the molasses and ketchup in a baking dish. Sprinkle with bacon bits and minced onion as desired.
2. Bake them for about 30 minutes at 350°.

Honey Sandwich Filling (serves 8)   Leslie Kuenzi[2]

3 tbsp. honey   4 oz. cream cheese

Beat the honey and cream cheese together until they are light and fluffy. For toast topping, add 4 tsp. orange juice, 1 tsp. orange peel and 1 tsp. pineapple juice to the filling. Makes 1 cup.

Vegetable Salad

Ruby Peebles[6]

1 box Knox gelatin
  (4 envelopes)
1 cup vinegar
½ cup pimento
1 tsp. salt

3 cups chopped celery
2 cups green peas
½ cup slivered almonds
1 medium green pepper(sliced)
3 chopped hard-boiled eggs

1. *Soak* Knox gelatin (all 4 envelopes) in one cup of cold water. *Dissolve* them in one cup of boiling water. Add 2 cups of cold water, 1 cup of vinegar, 1 cup of sugar, 1 teaspoon of salt.
2. When the gelatin mixture begins to set, add 3 cups of chopped celery, 2 cups of green peas, ½ cup of slivered almonds, ½ cup of pimento, and 1 medium green pepper.
3. Decorate the salad with 3 chopped hard-boiled eggs.

Baked Chicken

Lea Collins[6]

One 4-pound chicken or
  Two 2-pound cornish hens
Salt and pepper

Polyunsaturated margarine
2 teaspoons paprika
1 cup water or stock

Truss the chicken, then rub it with salt and pepper. Spread the breasts and thighs with margarine, place them on a rack in a baking pan; sprinkle them with paprika. Pour in stock or water. Bake the chicken in a moderately hot oven (350–425°) 1¼ hours or until the chicken is well browned and tender; baste it frequently. Add extra water to the pan during cooking if necessary.

Liberian Collard Greens

Murrey Dionne[6]

4 tablespoons cooking oil
10-oz. pack frozen collard
  greens
1 teaspoon minced onion
Pinch of black pepper
3 bouillon cubes (chicken
  flavored)

½ cup chopped chicken
½ cup of stew beef
¼ cup water
Medium heat

1. Place the oil, beef, ½ teaspoon onion, black pepper, and 1 bouillon cube in the pan and let brown.
2. Remove the beef.
3. Place the chicken in the pan and brown.
4. Remove the chicken.
5. Place the remaining ingredients in the pan, stirring them occasionally. When the collard greens turn from a light green color to darker green, place the beef and chicken back in the pan with all the ingredients.
6. Roll the ingredients together. Cover the pan and let it stand on low for approximately five minutes.
7. Serve it with rice.

Cheese and Broccoli Quiche   Debbie Gusler[6]

2 (9-inch) unbaked pie shells
slices of Swiss cheese
1 pkg. chopped broccoli
½ cup sliced mushrooms
  (optional)
1 can Tender Chunk Ham

3 eggs, beaten
1 cup Half and Half
2 teaspoons flour
½ teaspoon salt
¼ cup shredded cheddar cheese

Place the Swiss cheese on the bottom of the pie crust. Sprinkle it with broccoli, mushrooms and Tender Chunk Ham. Mix the next 4 ingredients. Pour them into pie shell. Sprinkle them with cheddar cheese. Bake it at 350° for 40–45 minutes.

Italian/Pasta Recipes

Hearty Spaghetti Sauce   John Goodin

1 large can tomato paste
1 large green pepper, chopped

2 large tomatoes, diced

1 large onion, chopped
4 oz. mushrooms sliced
  or pieces
Italian spices to your taste

1. Cook all the ingredients together until the onions and peppers are tender.
2. Ladle the sauce over cooked spaghetti or other pasta.

Pizza-Style Macaroni   Mary Vick[6]

½ lb. ground beef   ½ tsp. garlic salt
½ cup chopped onion   ½ tsp. basil
8-oz. small macaroni, cooked   ½ tsp. oregano
   and drained   6 oz. mozzarella cheese slices
2 8-oz. cans tomato sauce   (pepperoni and olives, optional)
¼ cup water

Brown the beef and onions together. Drain off the grease.
Mix them with the macaroni. Add 1 can of tomato sauce, water
and seasonings; toss them well. Top it with cheese, pepperoni and
olives.

Pour on the remaining tomato sauce. Bake it for 15–20 minutes at 375°. This is a great change from pizza and is much easier
to make. It can serve as the main dish for an Italian meal. It is
especially good with garlic toast.

Macaroni and Vegetable Salad   Donna Paris[6]

8-oz. package spiral macaroni   Italian dressing
Raw vegetables, chopped:
   tomatoes, carrots, onions,
   cucumbers, broccoli

1. Cook the macaroni according to the package directions.
2. Rinse the macaroni with cold water, then drain it.
3. Combine all the ingredients and toss them.
4. Chill it overnight.

Red Cole Slaw   Kay Payez[6]

¼ cup tomato soup (undiluted)   1 tablespoon oil
2 to 4 tablespoons sugar   ¼ tsp. salt, pepper, mustard
2 tablespoons vinegar

1. Bring the ingredients to a full boil and then cool them
down.

2. Pour the mixture over 2 cups shredded cabbage, ¼ green or red pepper (chopped) or chopped celery, and ½ cup drained canned tomatoes chopped (optional).

3. Chill it in the refrigerator.

Oriental Dishes

Occidental Stir-Fry (serves 4)   Bonnie Wilson[1]

1 20-oz. pkg. frozen, cut
  broccoli, thawed
3 tbsp. cold water
1 ½ tsp. cornstarch
3 tbsp. soy sauce
1 tsp. sugar

2 tbsp. cooking oil
1 cup celery, bias-sliced into
  ½-inch pieces
1 large onion cut into thin
  wedges

1. Thoroughly drain the thawed broccoli.

2. In a small bowl, combine the water and cornstarch. Stir in the soy sauce and sugar; then set it aside.

3. Heat a large skillet over high heat; add cooking oil. Then add celery, onion and broccoli.

4. Stir-fry the vegetables for about 5 minutes or until they are crisp-tender.

5. Stir the soy mixture, then stir it into the vegetables. Cook and stir the vegetables for about 1 minute more or until they are well coated. Serve them at once.

Sweet-and-Sour Sauce   Pennie Jayne Reece[2]

⅓ cup honey
⅓ cup pineapple juice
¼ cup vinegar

1 tbsp. soy sauce
1 tbsp. cornstarch

Combine all the ingredients in a saucepan and cook them until the starch sets.

Hot Chinese Chicken Stir Fry (serves 4)   Alta Cribb[6]

2–4 chicken breasts in 1" cubes
¼ cup cornstarch
¼ cup oil
⅛ tablespoon garlic powder
1 large tomato, cut up
1 4-oz. can water chestnuts
    drained and sliced

1 4-oz. can mushrooms (I use
    fresh ones)
½ cup chopped onions
1 cup celery, slant-sliced
1 tablespoon Accent (MSG)
¼ cup soy sauce
2 cups lettuce, finely shredded

1. Brown the chicken coated with cornstarch and garlic.
2. Add the other ingredients. Simmer them for 5 minutes.
3. Add the lettuce.
4. Serve it over rice.

Breads

Bran Pineapple Muffins   Dianne Marie Gibson[1]

1 cup wheat bran cereal
½ cup milk
1 cup crushed pineapple,
    drained
½ cup raisins
1 egg, beaten
½ cup brown sugar or
    ⅓ cup molasses

¼ cup vegetable oil or melted
    butter
1 cup whole-wheat flour
2 tsp. baking powder
½ tsp. salt
¼ tsp. baking soda

1. Preheat the oven to 400°.
2. Mix the bran, milk, pineapple and raisins; set them aside.
3. In a large mixing bowl, stir together the oil or melted butter and the egg; mix them well.
4. Mix the flour, baking powder, salt, baking soda and brown sugar. If you are using molasses, add it to the egg-oil mixture.
5. Blend all the ingredients, stirring them well.
6. Spoon the batter into 12 oiled muffin cups (fill them about ⅔ up) and bake them for 25 to 30 minutes.

Banana Nut Bread   Rosemary Billings and Sheila Eaddy[6]

½ cup shortening   1 tsp. soda
1 cup honey   3 large ripe bananas (1 cup)
2 eggs   ½ cup chopped nuts
2 cups whole-wheat graham   pinch of salt
  flour   1 tsp. vanilla

1. Cream the shortening, then add the honey. Beat in the eggs, one at a time. Sift together the flour, soda and salt. Stir them just enough to blend them. Add the bananas, vanilla and nuts.
2. Bake it in a loaf pan at 350° for about 1 hour. The bread will be a little more dense than normal.

Sour Cream Cornbread   Sherry Boykin[6]

1 ½ cups self-rising cornmeal   1 small can cream-style corn
1 egg   1 medium onion
½ cup cooking oil   1 cup sour cream

Combine the ingredients. Bake them at 350° until they are golden brown.

Beverages

Orange Drink (makes 4 8-oz. servings)   Pennie Jayne Reece[2]

1 cup milk   6 oz. frozen orange juice
1 cup water   1 tsp. vanilla
¼ cup honey

Mix the ingredients in a blender until the mixture is smooth. Then add 10 ice cubes and blend the mixture again.

Honey of a Punch (serves 16)   Pennie Jayne Reece[2]

½ cup honey   1 cup apple juice
3 cups hot water   1 pt. cranberry juice cocktail
6 oz. frozen lemonade

1. Blend the honey into the hot water. Let it stand until it's cool.
2. Mix in the remaining ingredients.
3. Chill the punch and pour it into a punch bowl. Garnish it with fruit ice cubes.

Hot Chocolate   Bettye Faulkner[6]

Mix 1 pkg. of Chocolate Milk Maker (Swiss Miss Sugar Free) with water and add Sweet and Low or saccharine and serve it hot (14 calories).

Milk Shakes   Bettye Faulkner[6]

Mix 1 pkg. of Swiss Miss Chocolate Milk Maker (Swiss Miss Sugar Free) with 1 cup of skim milk and lots of ice. Add several Sweet and Lows to taste and blend it in blender until it is like ice cream. You may add different flavoring to make different tastes (94 calories).

Desserts

My Favorite Coconut Cake   Sarah Goodin[1]

1 cup shortening	1 cup milk
2 cups sugar	1 egg
4 tsp. baking powder	1 tsp. vanilla
3 cups cake flour or all-purpose flour	

1. Cream the shortening, sugar and eggs for 2 minutes.
2. Add vanilla to the milk.
3. Mix the flour and baking powder.
4. Alternately add milk and the flour mix to the sugar-egg mix.
5. Bake the mix in 3 8" or 9" pans at 375° until they are done.
6. When the layers are cool, put them together with coconut filling.

Coconut Filling

3 cups sugar   1 ½ cups coconut milk or water
½ tsp. salt   1 grated or ground coconut

 1. Boil the sugar, salt, and coconut milk (or water) for 3 minutes.
 2. Add the coconut and boil the mixture 1 minute longer. Add vanilla (optional).
 3. Put in between layers.
 4. Frosting . . . use any standard "7 minute" frosting and sprinkle with coconut.

This *is* the world's best coconut cake! This is my mother's recipe. I realize that the recipe calls for some things we would generally do better to avoid, such as five cups of sugar. But remember: *you* are in control. You can choose to eat sweets from time to time, and you can choose to skip them. I'm including it to honor the greatest mom in the world . . . enough said.

—John Goodin

Easy Fruit Salad   Donna Paris[1]

2 8-oz. cans Mandarin oranges, drained 6 bananas, sliced
1 16-oz. can pineapple chunks 2 tbsp. Tang
1 16-oz. can light sliced peaches 1 pkg. vanilla instant pudding and pie mix

 1. Mix the oranges, undrained pineapple, undrained peaches and bananas in a large bowl. Add the dry ingredients and stir the mixture.
 2. Chill the fruit salad overnight.

Fruit Salad   Debbie Berry[1]

1 qt. strawberries, fresh or frozen 1 20-oz. can chunk pineapple
4 bananas, sliced ½ cup chopped pecans

1. Mix the ingredients together and chill the fruit salad before serving it.
2. (Optional) Serve it on top of vanilla ice cream.

Lime Ice Cream Dessert   Frances Hutson[1]

1 small pkg. lime gelatin
1 cup boiling water
1 pt. vanilla ice cream
1 cup chopped pecans

1 medium can crushed pineapple, drained
1 small jar Maraschino cherries, drained

1. Dissolve the gelatin in the boiling water.
2. Blend in the ice cream. Stir it until it melts. Stir in the remaining ingredients.
3. Pour the dessert into a mold and refrigerate it for several hours.

Honey-Rich Ice Cream (makes 4 qts.)   Pennie Jayne Reece[2]

5 eggs, separated
1 ½ cups honey
2 cups whipping cream
1 cup light cream

dash of salt
2 tbsp. vanilla
1 qt. milk

1. Beat the egg whites until they are stiff. Continue beating them as you slowly add the honey. Add well-beaten egg yolks, creams, salt and vanilla. Mix them well.
2. Pour the mix into a freezer container. Add enough milk to fill the container according to its directions.

Honey Queen's Fruit Dip   Leslie Kuenzi[2]

½ pt. lemon (or other flavor) yogurt

4 oz. cream cheese
1 tbsp. honey

1. Blend the ingredients until they are smooth.
2. Chill the dip, then serve it with your favorite fruits.

Honey Fruit Salad   Jean & Frank McKibbin[3]

6–8 cups fresh fruit   ½ cup honey
½ cup lemon juice   grated lemon rind (1 lemon)
1 egg, beaten   ½ cup whipping cream

1. Sprinkle the lemon juice over the fruit to prevent discoloration. Drain the excess juice before adding the dressing. Prepare dressing in steps 2–4.
2. Add the honey and lemon rind to the beaten egg (in a double boiler). Stir the mix until it thickens.
3. Chill the mixture.
4. Whip the cream until it is stiff, then fold it into the honey-and-egg mixture.
4. Pour the dressing over the fruit.

Honey Drops   Leslie Kuenzi[2]

1 cup powdered milk   1 cup peanut butter
1 cup graham cracker crumbs   1 cup raisins
1 cup honey

1. Combine the powdered milk and crumbs. Add the honey and mix it in.
2. Add the peanut butter and raisins, mixing them well.
3. Shape the mixture into balls. They may be dipped in chocolate or rolled in coconut.

Honey Pecan Pie   Pennie Jayne Reece[2]

3 eggs   ¼ tsp. salt
1 cup honey   1 cup pecans, coarsely chopped
1 tsp. vanilla extract   1 tsp. melted butter, cooled
1 unbaked pie shell, chilled

1. Beat the eggs until they are foamy. Continue beating them while adding honey in a fine stream.

2. Beat in the vanilla, butter and salt. Add pecans.

3. Pour the mixture into a pie shell.

4. Bake the pie at 400° for 10 minutes. Then reduce heat to 300°.

5. Bake the pie at 300° for 20 minutes. Then reduce heat to 250°.

6. Bake the pie at 250° for 10 minutes or until the filling is firm.

Whipped Cream with Honey   Pennie Jayne Reece[2]
 (makes 2 1/4 cups)

1 cup (1/2 pt.) whipping cream 1 tsp. vanilla
2 tbsp. mild honey

1. Chill beaters, bowl and the cream.

2. Whip the cream until soft peaks form. Slowly beat in the honey and vanilla.

Chilled Cheesecake   Pennie Jayne Reece[2]

1 3-oz. pkg. lemon gelatin 1 tsp. vanilla
1/2 cup boiling water   1 1/2 cups evaporated milk,
8 oz. cream cheese   chilled
1/2 cup honey   1 graham cracker crust
2 tsp. lemon juice

1. Mix the gelatin in the boiling water until the gelatin dissolves. Chill it until it has partially set.

2. Mix the cheese with the honey, lemon juice and vanilla.

3. Whip the chilled milk until it is stiff; then fold it into the cheese mixture. Combine it with the gelatin.

4. Pour the mix into the graham cracker crust. Chill it before serving.

Rice Pudding (serves 8)   Leslie Kuenzi[2]

2 cups cooked rice   3 cups milk
¾ cup honey   1 cup raisins, chopped
3 eggs

    1. Mix the rice, milk and honey.
    2. Slightly beat the eggs and add them to the rice mixture.
    3. Stir in the raisins.
    4. In a well-greased baking dish, bake the pudding at 350°
for 1 hour. Serve it with cream (optional).

Leslie's Honey Chocolate Bars   Leslie Kuenzi[2]

4 cups Rice Krispies   1 6-oz. pkg. butterscotch chips
¾ cup honey   ½ cup peanut butter
1 6-oz. pkg. chocolate chips

    1. Heat the cereal in a shallow pan at 350° for 10 minutes.
At the same time, bring the honey to a simmer over low heat.
    2. Remove the honey from the heat and add the chips.
    3. Pour the cereal into a greased bowl and pour the chips
and honey over the cereal. Stir the mix until the cereal is well
coated.
    4. With your hands, pat the mixture into a 7″ × 11″ pan and
chill it.

Natural Carrot Cake   Dianne Gibson[6]

1 ½ cups honey   2 tsp. soda
4 eggs, well beaten   2 tsp. ground cinnamon
2 cups whole wheat flour   1 cup chopped pecans
1 tsp. salt   1 ½ cups oil
3 cups grated carrots

    Mix the honey and oil. Add the eggs, mixing them well, then
sift and add all the dry ingredients. Mix until smooth. Add the

nuts and carrots. Bake them in long pan at 325° for 50 minutes or until a toothpick comes out clean.

Frozen Yogurt Ideas   Courtesy of TCBY[4]

Yogurt is a natural milk product that is both healthful and satisfying. It contains calcium, phosphorous, riboflavin and protein, along with B vitamins, iron, zinc, magnesium and panothenic acid. It is also economical—it can be purchased in large quantities (a gallon or more).

It can be used as a substitute for ice cream in desserts such as sundaes, pies and milk shakes. Skim milk and two scoops of your favorite frozen yogurt mixed in a blender makes a great shake! It also makes a delicious snack when topped with fresh fruit, sandwiched between waffles or wrapped up in crepes.

Peanut Recipes[5]

Peanut Facts

Peanuts . . .
—are 26 percent protein
—contain no cholesterol (cholesterol comes from foods of animal origin) and are low in saturated fat
—qualify as a low-sodium food (one ounce of unsalted peanuts contains 1.6 milligrams of sodium; a teaspoon of salt contains 2,132 milligrams of sodium)
—supply dietary fiber or roughage valuable in the body's waste-elimination process

Peanut Hints

Peanut Storage: To maintain the best eating quality, store your peanuts in a cool, dry place, at or below 70° F. Peanuts will stay fresh indefinitely in a tightly closed container in a freezer.

Types to Use in Recipes: Recipes specify when raw peanuts are to be used and indicate the type required—in the shell; shelled redskins; or shelled blanched (with the redskins removed). When roasted peanuts are called for, the home-roasted (without redskins), commercial cocktail or dry roasted peanuts may be used interchangeably. Some recipes call for roasted peanuts with the redskins.

Peanut Butter in Recipes: Either homemade peanut butter (of a consistency comparable to commercial peanut butter), old-fashioned nonstabilized or regular commercial stabilized peanut butter may be used. If chunky (crunchy) peanut butter is required, the recipe will say so.

Chopping Peanuts: Peanuts are easily chopped in a food processor, or by dropping a few at a time into a blender, or with an inexpensive nut chopper.

How Many Peanuts? Approximately 1½ pounds of raw, unshelled peanuts equals 1 pound of raw shelled peanuts or 3¼ cups. Approximately 5 ounces of raw shelled peanuts equal 1 cup. Approximately 12 ounces of roasted shelled peanuts equal 2 cups.

Peanut Seafood Salad

3 cups cooked rice, chilled
1 12¾ oz. can of tuna (or
   shrimp or crab)
2 hard-cooked eggs, chopped
   or sliced

2 large tomatoes, cut into
   wedges
1 cup roasted peanuts, chopped
¼ cup lemon juice
¼ cup bell pepper, chopped

1. In a large salad bowl, toss together the rice, tuna, chopped eggs, tomatoes, peanuts, pepper and lemon juice.
2. Serve the salad plain or with the Special French Dressing.

Special French Dressing

½ cup peanut oil
¼ cup white vinegar
1 clove garlic, crushed

½ tsp. salt
¼ tsp. oregano

Place all the ingredients in a screw-top container and shake it vigorously. Allow it to stand about 15 minutes. Serve it at room temperature.

Magnificent Mandarin Salad (serves 4 to 6)

1 cup orange or plain yogurt	1 tsp. salt (optional)
1 tbsp. honey	1 tsp. black pepper (optional)
2 carrots, grated	3 leaves lettuce or watercress
2 large apples, chopped	1 can (11 oz.) Mandarin oranges,
2 stalks celery, finely chopped	drained
1 cup roasted peanuts	

1. Mix the yogurt and honey.
2. Fold in the vegetables, nuts and fruits.
3. Add seasoning (optional).
4. Chill the salad (optional).
5. Serve it on a bed of lettuce or watercress.

Banana and Peanut Butter Sandwich

bread	2 tbsp. peanut butter
1 banana	

Spread one slice of bread with peanut butter. Then slice a banana on top.

Honey and Peanut Butter Sandwich

bread	2 tbsp. peanut butter
1 ½ tsp. honey	

Mix the honey and peanut butter and spread on one slice of bread.

Raisin and Peanut Butter Sandwich

bread   2 tbsp. peanut butter
2 tbsp. raisins, chopped

Mix the peanut butter and the chopped raisins; spread it on a slice of bread.

Crunchy Combo (serves 18 to 20)

1 cup roasted peanuts   1 cup dried apple pieces, diced
1 cup seedless raisins   1 6-oz. pkg. chocolate chips

1. Toss the ingredients in a bowl until they are thoroughly mixed.
2. Store the mixture in a tightly closed container.

Crunchy Ham Rolls (makes 48)

8 oz. cream cheese   1 clove garlic, minced
1 cup roasted peanuts, finely 12 thin slices boiled ham
  chopped   48 round crackers

1. Combine the cream cheese, peanuts and garlic.
2. Spread each slice of ham with the mixture. Roll them up.
3. Chill them thoroughly.
4. Cut them into slices, and serve each slice on a round cracker.

Nutty Tomato Stack-Ups (serves 8)

½ cup roasted peanuts,   1 10-oz. pkg. frozen broccoli,
  chopped   chopped
4 large tomatoes   2 tbsp. onion, finely chopped
1 cup (4 oz.) Swiss cheese,
  shredded

1. Cook the broccoli according to the directions on the package; drain it.

2. Add the cheese, onion and peanuts, stirring them well.

3. Cut the tomatoes in half and place them cut side up in a baking dish.

4. Spoon the broccoli mixture onto each tomato half.

5. Broil them 5 inches from the heat for 8 minutes or until the cheese melts.

Peanut Egg Rolls

1 lb. pork sausage (bulk)
1 lb. lean ground beef
1 large onion, chopped
peanut oil for deep frying

2 cups roasted peanuts, chopped
1 pkg. Chinese egg roll
  wrappers
2 cups sharp cheese, shredded

1. Brown the meats and onion, then drain off all the grease.

2. Mix in the cheese and peanuts.

3. Fill the eggroll wrappers according to the package directions.

4. Deep-fry the eggrolls until they are golden brown.

5. Serve them with your favorite hot mustard or sweet-and-sour sauce.

P-Nutty Fingers (makes 48)

12 slices bread
1 cup milk
1 cup flaked coconut

2 cups roasted peanuts, finely
  chopped
½ cup peanut butter

1. Trim the crusts from the bread. Cut each slice into fingers about ½ inch wide.

2. Blend the milk and peanut butter.

3. In a separate container, toss together the chopped peanuts and coconut.

4. Dip the pieces of bread into the butter-and-milk mixture, then roll them in the peanut-and-coconut mix and place them on a baking sheet.

5. Bake them in a preheated oven at 400° for about 8 minutes or until they are lightly browned.

Honey Peanut Butter Balls (makes 48)

½ cup honey
1 cup dry milk

1 cup roasted peanuts, chopped
½ cup creamy peanut butter

1. Pour the peanuts into a plate or shallow bowl and set them aside.

2. In a medium-sized bowl, combine the peanut butter and honey. Stir in the dry milk, mixing it well.

3. Form the dough into balls about an inch in diameter. Roll each ball in the peanuts until it is well coated.

Double Peanut Clusters (makes 24)

⅓ cup creamy peanut butter
1 cup roasted peanuts,
   blanched or with redskins

6 oz. semi-sweet chocolate bits

1. Melt the chocolate bits and the peanut butter in the top of a double boiler over hot (not boiling) water. Stir them until they are blended.

2. Add the peanuts and stir the mixture until they are coated.

3. Drop teaspoonfuls onto waxed paper and chill the clusters until they are firm.

Jiffy Goober Haystacks (makes 36)

6 oz. butterscotch morsels
1 cup roasted peanuts

⅓ cup creamy peanut butter
3 oz. chow mein noodles

1. Melt the butterscotch morsels and peanut butter in the top of a double boiler over hot (not boiling) water. Stir them until they are blended.

2. Add the peanuts and noodles and stir the mix until the noodles and nuts are well covered.

3. Form clusters of the mix on waxed paper and allow them to harden.

Notes

1. From the cookbook produced by the Ladies Fellowship of New Covenant Life Baptist Church, P.O. Box 538, Knightdale, NC 27545.

2. Courtesy of the American Beekeeping Federation, 13637 NW 39th Ave., Gainesville, FL 32606.

3. From *Cookbook of Foods from Bible Days,* Jean and Frank McKibbin.

4. TCBY, 1100 TCBY Tower, 425 W. Capitol Ave., Little Rock, AR 72201.

5. The peanut hints and the peanut recipes are provided courtesy of Growers Peanut Food Promotions, P.O. Box 1709, Rocky Mount, NC 27802.

6. Courtesy of the individuals submitting the recipes.

An exciting idea was born in my life!

14

U.B.I.C.
Principle Posters

The next two pages are your U.B.I.C. Principle posters.

Put one on the door of your refrigerator.
Put the other poster on the dash of your car.

The posters are friendly reminders that you're in charge of your life . . . that your body does not control you . . . that you're developing an exciting new life style . . . that you're on your way to a new you—a slimmer, healthier person.

Remember the U.B.I.C. Principle!
"You Be In Control!"

We want to know of your success in losing weight. Please contact the author:

Dr. John Goodin
P.O. Box 20003
Raleigh, N.C. 27619

Remember the U.B.I.C. Principle

"YOU BE IN CONTROL!"

A SLIMMER, HEALTHIER YOU IS ON THE WAY.

THAT'S EXCITING!

Remember the U.B.I.C. Principle

"YOU
BE
IN
CONTROL!"

A SLIMMER, HEALTHIER YOU IS ON THE WAY.

THAT'S EXCITING!

A SUMMARY OF THE BENEFITS AND FEATURES OF YOUR WEIGHT LOSS PROGRAM:

- Teaches you how to adopt a new, healthier lifestyle.
- Enhances your self-discipline.
- Helps you to be goals-oriented.
- Gives you a way to express and establish your motivation in "black and white" in writing.
- Eat real, delicious food.
- No counting calories.
- No weighing or measuring food portions.
- No gimmicks — no magic pills or potions.
- Inexpensive — nothing special or extra to buy except this book.
- Feel great about yourself!
- Works whether you need to lose ten pounds or hundreds of pounds.
- Weight loss maintenance is a natural part of your new lifestyle.
- You're not on a "diet," you're learning a new, exciting way to live.
- No meal replacement beverages.
- No diet pills.
- No special packaged foods.
- No starving yourself.